THE LIFE STORY OF
ROBERT J.
LOVELACE

Baby Robert and his older sister

THE LIFE STORY OF

ROBERT J. LOVELACE

Southwestern Virginia, Appalachia

ROBERT J. LOVELACE

Lovelace
P.O. Box 20683
Roanoke, VA 24018

Printed in the United States of America

ISBN: 979-8-9869031-0-1

First Edition

10 9 8 7 6 5 4 3 2 1

THIS BOOK IS DEDICATED TO
MY FAMILY & CHURCH.

Thank you for the support you have given me in my later years. May you live a long and fulfilling life. I greatly appreciate my daughter, Debra's, and Jay Kincanon's assistance with this autobiography. This book is also dedicated to teachers, those in military service, and people everywhere who offer a helping hand to others. Your work is noble.

INTRODUCTION

Memory betrays us all, such as: The face is familiar, but what was the name? Where did we go? What did we say? When did it happen? As cognitive memory begins around the age of three, I assume that some of what I say here started around the age of three or four. I read somewhere that one remembers what he remembered from the last time he thought on the same subject.

Having lived 97 years, I find myself belonging to a generation obsessed with retaining and relaying everything. I now understand the better things of the past were not so often articles or possessions accumulated as they were the manners in which people lived, the things they thought and the time in which they lived. This, of course, is still true. The fine things and modern way we live today will be different in a very few years hence. For some reason I have always wanted to write of my past to provide a description of a different time and to leave a record of my life's challenges and stresses for those who come after me. None of my memories are confabulations. It seems to depress me somewhat as I try to remember the past. I do not know the reason for this feeling but be it as it may, I am compelled to write.

CHAPTER I

TROUTDALE, VIRGINIA

Troutdale was located on the covered-wagon route in Grayson County between Marion, Virginia and Ash County, North Carolina. It had a population of about twenty-eight hundred or more at the time of my birth. Before that it had been a small settlement since 1870. It was incorporated by the Virginia General Assembly on March 12, 1906 making it the highest incorporated town in Virginia with an eleva-

Homeplace in snow

Recent homeplace with Robert

tion of 3,700 feet, and located near Mount Rogers, the tallest mountain in Virginia, at 5,729 feet. Passengers could ride the old Marion & Rye Railway into Troutdale until the 1930s.

The town was laid out in a one mile circle the center being the northwest corner of the Methodist Church lot. Grayson County was formed out of Wythe County in 1793 based on a book Pioneer Settlers of Grayson Co., VA.[1] It was a lumber boom town with a Vaudeville theater, a bank, a US post office, a telephone office and a cattle yard that was located in the western part of the township. It also had a furniture factory, three churches, two barber shops, two produce houses, two ice cream parlors, a hat shop, Masonic Hall, several hotels, restaurants, a high school, a blacksmith shop, a grist mill, a feed store, clothing and dry goods stores, a carpenter shop that made caskets, a train station, a taxi, and a newspaper: *The Troutdale News*. There was a plant to extract tannic acid from the bark of chestnut oak and eastern hemlock for the tanning of leather which was used by the United States Leather Company. The Grayson Lumber Company in nearby Fairwood produced more than 125,000 feet of hardwood per day. The Phoenix Iron Ore Company was also there. Other small stores existed as typical of the day. In the 1920s Troutdale became a summer tourist resort. As I remember it, the theater was not in use. It had been closed long before my time. Steve Long owned it and used it for a storage warehouse and a grist mill. I think the Perkins Department store was the largest and was owned by Breeze and Hattie Perkins. The Perkins family owned most of the property in and around Troutdale, including large dairy barns and farm land in all directions. They controlled the cattle business in this part of Grayson County. They sold out and went to California sometime in the early nineteen thirties.

ELECTRICITY

Troutdale had its own electric power plant. There was a dam on Fox Creek with a raceway that ran around the side of the hill to the place where the water ran down a chute to a turbine wheel that powered the generators to produce the electricity. As the story goes, in later years the owner-operator only ran the power plant when he saw fit.

ENTERTAINMENT IN TROUTDALE

Times were hard and there was little extra money in the Lovelace budget for entertainment. Sometimes on weekends we went to Mr. and Mrs. Leonard's house in Troutdale to listen to the radio for entertainment.

The only moving picture show that could be seen without going to Marion was someone would show old movies on Saturday night using the side of the Primitive Baptist Church as a screen when the weather was good. Sometimes the power would go off. If the weather was bad there was no show. Sometimes they had a good excuse for the power failure when the creek was low on water. The only compensation the operator got was from selling popcorn and candy. There was no admission charge.

The circus would come to town occasionally. I would volunteer to help the animal attendant to water and feed the animals. The attendant would go around back and slip me in under the tent as payment for helping. I don't know if the show manager knew this or not. Maybe I was doing the attendant's job for him. I really didn't care how I got in, only that I did.

CHAPTER 2

ROBERT CARY & BESSIE JOINES LOVELACE FAMILY

I was born into this world on September 9, 1925 at the home of Robert Cary (b. March 15, 1880, d. March 27, 1971) and Bessie Joines (b. June 10, 1900, d. August 16, 1980) Lovelace. I was the second of seven children. My brothers and sisters were in order of birth: Margaret Elizabeth, Robert (me), Irene and Ilene (the twins), Grady Wayne, Donald Zane and

Bessie May Joines Lovelace Age 10 with her older sister

Mary Patsy. Also, I have six half sisters and one half brother. My father was married twice. My father's first wife died in the early nineteen hundreds during the great influenza epidemic. My life began in an eight room white farm house encircled with a white wooden picket fence located on top of a hill about one mile west of the hamlet town of Troutdale.

At the time of my birth, large farming families were customary to help with the work and chores. My arrival came just before the great depression into a family already saddled with poverty.

MEMORIES OF MY MOTHER

My mother was a beautiful, resourceful and hard working woman. Not only did she keep the house and cook for a large family, she assisted my father in the fields, kept up the housework, and pinched pennies from herbs that she would garden and sell at Reedy's Produce Store. My Mother was a very short person about four foot eight but was a giant in all other ways. She was a kind and gentle person who never seemed to show her worries or temper. I feel very fortunate to have had a mother like her. I don't recall ever seeing her mad or upset. Well, maybe a few times when she spanked me for misbehaving. I tried to run from her one time and she told me she would follow me all the way to Marion so I stopped and sat down near the barn on a big round limestone rock and began to cry. I suppose she spanked me I don't remember. She was well thought of and liked by everyone in the community. Without her love, correction and nurturing, I don't know where I would be today. I could never repay her for the many things that she did for me. One thing she taught me was not to steal. Once I took a piece of chalk from the Mitchell's home (a neighbor) without permission. Mother discovered what I had done and she made me take the chalk back and apologize to Mrs. Mitchell. I will never forget that as long as I live. Never have I taken anything without permission since.

MEMORIES OF MY FATHER

My father was a hard working and short tempered man of faith who would read his Bible almost every night. On Sundays, he would read the Bible aloud for at least an hour but he would never make us listen to him if we did not want too. Many times he would get an old hymn book and sing with my sister Margaret songs like "The Old Rugged Cross", "We will Understand it All By and By", "How Beautiful Heaven Must Be" and many others. When I close my eyes and concentrate, it seems as though I can hear them singing those old songs even today. He would never work on Sunday even when threatened with the potential loss of crops. When he could find work outside the farm, it was generally painting a house or some other odd job. Prior to using lead paint, he would swallow a little arsenic to prevent becoming sick from the lead. My father's fee for his work was a whopping ten cents per hour. He was opposed to welfare and would not accept charity of any kind.

He also cut and sold firewood to the town folks for one dollar and fifty cents per face cord[2]. The wood was split to no larger than about two and one half inch diameter. He would go to the person's house and measure the fire box of the stove and then he would cut each piece of wood exactly to match it. The wood had to be cut with what was called a "cross cut" saw. This saw had to have a person on each end of it to saw. I think a one man cross cut saw was available but he never owned one. He always had one horse to work the farm and haul wood and one cow for milk and butter.

I can't remember how old I was, but one year about a week before Christmas, my father got up before daylight and tried to leave the house without waking us. But I heard him and found out that he was going to Marion which was about eighteen miles away. I begged to go with him and he finally said okay! Eighteen miles over a gravel road in a wagon is a long way for a child but I enjoyed being with and going places with my Father. He was going to buy some candy and other small things to stuff our stockings for Santa Clause. We arrived in Marion that afternoon and he left me in the wagon to guard the chestnuts and other things he was going to sell. After he finished with business, we started for Troutdale. We got as far as the little settlement of Attaway before nightfall. We stopped and spent the night with a friend of my father, Mr. Gallagher. I remember it well because I fell out of bed that night. I wasn't hurt but was greatly embarrassed. The trip was a great learning experience because along the way my father explained lots of his own life situations; many of which I too would come to experience. On this trip I found out "THERE WAS NO SANTA CLAUSE!" I was disappointed but now I knew something that the other kids didn't which made me feel very grown-up. We arrived back in Troutdale the next day.

When I was about twelve years old, my Mother and I went to town. She bought something at Boss Paisley's country store. On the way home I came to the conclusion that Boss had cheated her on some change. Without Mother's knowledge, I returned to the store and confronted Boss and asked him for the difference. He became very upset at me and came from behind the counter and slapped me on my left ear rupturing my ear drum. My mother didn't know I had gone back to the store. I went to my father who was doing some carpenter work in town and told him what had happened. Boss knew he had done something wrong and he knew my father would come looking for him so he closed the store and went upstairs where he lived and locked the door.

My father was one who would not allow anyone big or small to mess with anyone in his family, so he took his claw hammer and went looking for Boss. I guess it was a good thing that he did not find him. My Father left Troutdale and went to the courthouse in Independence, VA and got a warrant for Boss' arrest. My Father took me to the doctor and he confirmed that my ear drum was ruptured but that it should heal. A good friend named Harry Anderson came a few days later and talked my Father into dropping the charges against Boss. Nonetheless, I had a ringing in my ear for a couple of months before all healed.

When my paternal grandfather, William Lovelace, passed away my father and I took his casket and remains in a buck-board wagon back to his family cemetery in NC. It had recently rained hard and flooded parts of the cemetery road. As we moved down the road, the water flowed into the buck-board and the casket rose up and began to float in the wagon. Through my father's strength and quick thinking, he held the reins and grabbed the casket while directing me to assist. Together we were able to keep the casket from floating away and reach the family plot for my grandfather's burial.

MY PARENTS LAID A FOUNDATION

In this day and time we're frequently hearing of someone blaming their parents for their own deficiencies in life because of some abuse or mistreatment as a child. We surely had it hard back in Troutdale but I cannot blame my parents for our poverty in those days nor can I blame them that we had less than most other families. They shared the same amount of love, care and consideration for each of us. I believe that I have a better outlook on life and appreciate what I do have because of the way I was raised. I was taught to save and not to waste anything, to eat everything on my plate and to take only what I could eat! I was taught never to lie to anyone about anything even if telling the truth meant I could get into trouble. I was also taught the "Golden Rule", to treat everyone like I would have them treat me.

I recall being baptized and joining Fox Creek Mountain Baptist Church when I was about 17 years old. The family had to walk about two miles to attend church services. The church would seat about 50 people. Fox Creek was a one-room church with a wood burning stove in the center of the pews. We did not have nor would the church allow any

Robert's parents 1960s

musical instruments including piano and organ. We were only privy to one pastor led church service per month since the pastor also had 3 to 4 congregations at other locations and was responsible for their services. Church business was handled on select Saturdays and Bible study was held on Sundays. Sunday church lasted about 2 hours. Our church did not have Sunday school but I think most other churches in the area did. I recall each year the church held a week-long revival. It was "all day preaching and dinner on the ground!" In other words, the multiple preachers spoke at length and there was a large outdoor pot luck meal with church members and visitors. Watermelon was eaten by holding a slice between your hands and informal competitions occurred of who could spit the seeds the farthest.

In summary, in growing-up in the Lovelace household I believe my Mother and Father laid an almost perfect foundation in those days of depression and poverty to overcoming life's issues and obstacles. I can only say that as I look back on those early years of

my life that I was very blessed and that I'm extremely
thankful to God for placing me in their care.

MOTHER & FATHER'S PASSING

Mother

I attribute the betterment in my life mostly to Mother.
If I were to take the time and make space here to
tell you all the great and kind things Mother did
for children and others who knew her, there would
be neither room nor time left to finish this writing.
On top of her other responsibilities, she took care of
Mrs. Pruitt (who was bed ridden) for many years in
our home, feeding and bathing her because she did
not have a place to go. Later in life Mother's physical
strength and desire to live supported her when she
was alone and fell outside the farmhouse in freezing
weather and broke her hip. Mother dragged herself
across the yard and was able to open the farmhouse
door to reach a phone and call for help. Her grit

was the reason she did not freeze and was able to have surgery and walk again. Mother died at age eighty on August 16, 1980. She was highly esteemed in the community as evidenced by the turnout for her viewing. Although the population of Troutdale at that time was only around 350, more than 400 came in respect and tribute to a woman who loved and gave much to her family and community. Over several lifetimes, I could never repay her for what she did that helped me forge my values, sense of responsibility and life.

Father

According to my mother, my father was never considered to be an "old man!" He was good at playing the organ and violin, could read music and was a great debater. He played a tremendous part in helping to create my mechanical aptitude and work ethic. My Father died at age ninety one on March 27, 1971. In my eyes he was a giant of a man and father.

FARM-LIFE

How well I remember the old two story farmhouse where I was born. Early on the non-electrified house sat on top of a hill west of Troutdale about one-tenth of a mile off the dirt road that went northward toward Marion, VA. This beautiful old house was painted white, trimmed in green and could be seen for miles. I can still remember those bright sunny days where the blades of grass seemed to sway as the breezes would come through the trees around the house. The property also sported a large log barn with an attached lean-to style sheep shed, a chicken house, a two-story tobacco barn and a large granary and a small tenant house. All activities after sunset were done by the light of a kerosene lamp or lantern.

OUR WATER SUPPLY

Our water was plentiful and came from a forty-five foot deep hand-dug well which was covered by an eight by twelve-foot well-house. Our milk and butter was kept in a milk-trough where cool well water was hand pumped into the trough to reduce spoilage. On warm days the water in the milk-trough had to be changed twice daily to prevent the milk from spoiling. A grape vine and chicken wire covered much of the well-house. The grape vine helped keep the well-house cool in the summer.

SHARECROPPING

Not only were we poor but our farmland for growing crops was very poor as well. The farm covered about fifty acres. However, the poor land required fertilizer which we really couldn't afford. We improvised using horse and cow manure from the barn and chip litter from the woodshed. One sign of a family's poverty was if their lively-hood came from sharecropping and we were sharecroppers. As sharecroppers during the summer months we walked from two to four miles each way, every day except Sunday just to get to the farmland. When we arrived back at the house after farming each evening, we then had to complete our chores at home. Many times our arrival back home was after dark which meant that our chores had to be completed using lanterns. Some of the fields we farmed were on rolling land in the Anderson Hill or Rocky Hollow section of Grayson County and others were on mountainside land. Parts of the land were so steep that one could hardly stand up on it.

The corn had to be cut by hand and put into shocks; then, when dried it was shucked by hand and hauled to the granary. Corn fodder was stacked and in the winter fed to the cow. The wheat, rye, oats and buckwheat were harvested with a grain cradle, tied in bundles and shucked. When dry, the bundles were hauled to a central spot and put in stacks. The exception to this process was buckwheat which could not be stacked because in drying most of the grain would just fall-off. Therefore, buckwheat had to be thrashed as soon as it was dry. The stacking of hay and grains was made by putting a pole in the ground which reached upward to 10-15 feet above the ground. The grain bundles were placed around it with the top of the grain facing the pole to protect it from the weather. They were all put in a convenient flat spot so the thrashing machine would have access to them when time came. A smaller crop like buckwheat was thrashed by hand using a flail[3]. The grain to be thrashed was usually put on a tarpaulin and hit with the flail to release the chaff and then winnowed.[4]

PUTTING-UP HAY
FOR WINTER

A team of horses was used to pull a mowing machine to cut the hay. The hay was then allowed to dry in the field, raked into rows with a two horse rake, and by hand using a hay fork, the hay was cut into small shocks. The final step was loading the hay on a wagon or dragging it with a chain or rope by horse to the barn or after the barn was filled to some other convenient location. Hay not placed in the barn was put into a stack with a tapered "hay-cap" to shed water. Hay could be bailed but for us that was too costly.

I remember once when a farmer (Mr. Jarvis) asked my father if I could plow a three-acre field for him that he intended to sow in buckwheat. It was June and very hot but my Father told him that I could go with him and plow. Mr. Jarvis picked me up early the next morning and took me to Sugar Grove to his brother's farm. Upon seeing my small stature Mr. Jarvis' brother said, "My God, I thought you were bringing someone to plow." Like my father I've always had a short-temper and was insulted by his remark! Jarvis' brother had a team of four-year-old horses with each horse weighing about eighteen-hundred pounds. I plowed all morning with a large No. 40 Oliver turn plow. I did not stop to let the team rest so by twelve o'clock the horses were white with sweat lather. At about 1 P.M., after a short lunch-break when it came time for me to start plowing again, Mr. Jarvis came to me and very quietly asked me to take it easy on the horses. I told him that I heard his brother's remark that morning about my size and he apologized. I plowed the rest of that day but I never did any further plowing for Mr. Jarvis.

CLOGGED WATER PIPE

Water was piped into the house from a spring about one-tenth mile away.

I know the distance well because about 1942, I decided to dig up the pipe to clean-out the silt that was blocking the water flow. In some places I had to dig as deep as five feet around the side of a hill to uncover the pipe. All digging was with a pick and shovel. I would throw the dirt up the hill above the ditch so it would be easier to back-fill the ditch once the pipe was cleaned. In cleaning each 20-ft. joint I tied a cloth on one end to a strong-stiff wire. As the wire was pulled through each joint the cloth would swab the pipe clean. On occasion the swab would get stuck resulting in my having to chain one end of the pipe to a fence post. I then hooked our horse to the wire and she had no trouble pulling the wire through the pipe. It took quite awhile to clean the 500-ft. of pipe but completion brought us good clean water. Success was short-lived. In order to keep silt out of the pipe required that we concrete the sides and bottom of the spring. Since we did not have money for concrete the pipes again filled with silt and became inoperable. A hand dug well was subsequently installed. It worked very well for many years before it began to run dry. My Mother had a new well bored that is still in operation. All that's left of the old well-house today is its protective well cover.

FEEDING THE FAMILY

Selling Meat and Produce

Being poor is a frame of mind. We didn't realize that we were very poor but we did know that we

Robert and his three sisters early 1930s

Robert and his siblings late 1940s

were rich in many ways. It took a lot of work to feed the family. During the summer we raised money by picking wild blackberries and blueberries (huckleberries). I remember that the blackberries were used primarily in the making of wine, and that the blueberries brought about thirty cents per gallon. We raised turkeys to sell which brought-in about twenty-five to thirty dollars a year. We also raised two hogs each year that were butchered in the fall for the ham.

Our Food Supply

There was an orchard with about twenty-five apple trees, one tall damson tree, a cherry tree, and a pear tree. There was a large chestnut tree that stood on the hill above the house that our turkeys used to roost in. On occasion an owl would take a turkey for his meal.

Each year mother would plant a large garden with tomatoes, potatoes, beets, sweet corn, cabbage, parsnips, rutabaga, cucumbers and beans. The date of the planting occurred based on the position of the moon and by referencing the Almanac. She canned a lot of vegetables from the garden. She also made apple butter from the apples in the orchard. Vegetables such as potatoes, beets, parsnips, rutabaga, could be buried in a straw lined hole dug in the ground and covered with corn fodder to preserve freshness. Cabbage was buried upside down with the roots above ground. They could be dug up even when frozen in the ground and they would be as fresh as when they were buried. Apples could be dried on a homemade evaporator and a furnace made of stones and mud.[5] The evaporator was set on top of the furnace, a fire was put under it for heat which in turn dried the apples. I guess that one could say that the apples were steam dried.

My mother churned sour cream and made butter. She kept the sour buttermilk from the churn to make biscuits and cornbread. It was also good to drink or mix with cornbread. She could take almost nothing and make a good meal of it. She would make what was called "depression gravy" for breakfast each morning. A depression gravy or "white sop" was made by using hog side meat grease mixed with flour and milk and boiled in an iron skillet until it thickened. This gravy was very good on hot biscuits. I still love it.

Molasses

We always raised some cane to make molasses. The cane had to be stripped of its foliage and the top cut off then it was cut down and hauled to the cane mill. The cane foliage was tied in bundles and fed to the cow in the winter. The cane heads were taken to a hammer mill[6] and processed for feed for the cow also. This was done just before the first frost. If the cane got frostbit it would not make good molasses. The cane was rolled between two and sometimes three large rollers set in an upright frame with cogs on the top end.[7] We also made cane molasses on the same furnace that was used to dry apples. The molasses pan was made somewhat like the evaporator except it did not have a top. It had a horse shoe fastened to each corner so a pole or iron bar could be inserted across the front and back and with four people it could easily be removed from the furnace. The cane juice was boiled and skimmed constantly to remove the green foam that gathered on it. After it was boiled down to a certain thickness, it was removed from the fire and strained through a cheese-cloth strainer. It was then stored in fruit jars or in crock pots. It was now called cane molasses. Usually the making of molasses lasted two or three days. It varied according as to how much cane was to be processed. We would start early in the morning and work well into the night. This is where all the fun came in. All of us children along with the neighbor's children would gather and play games until the molasses making would quit for the night.

Meat

Our meat consisted primarily of wild-game like rabbit, squirrel and turkey. The better parts of the hogs we raised, except for the hams, became part of our food supply. Our hog meat was preserved through either canning or salt-curing.

OUR FIREPLACE

We loved to roast potatoes in the hot embers in our open fireplace. Wild chestnuts could be roasted the same way except one must cut a little hole in the shell or it would explode sending fire and ashes all over the room. One could roast apples in front of the fire place by attaching a string to the mantle over the fireplace and then attaching an apple to the string by its stem, adjust the apple to the right place in front of the fire, then wind up the string very tight and turn it loose. In the process of unwinding it would roast the apple evenly all around. When the string unwound the apple would have enough momentum to wind the string up in the opposite direction. This would continue until the string would completely unwind. We roasted potatoes by putting them in the hot ashes at the front of the fireplace. Ears of sweet corn could be roasted in the same way as the apples or it could be set near the fire and rotated ever so often by hand.

CLOTHING

During the great depression, Mother made most all of our clothing from store bought cloth and flax. During those years when holes appeared in britches, shirts and socks they were patched. At school I gained the honor of being called "rag man" from the other children. In the fall each of us children received a new pair of shoes. My father had to work nine hours to pay the 90 cent price for a pair of our shoes so they had to last a full year. My Father frequently worked on our shoes to insure they lasted through the winter. He would re-sole, re-heel and sew them as needed. One year he even made me a pair of leather shoes which didn't fit well. I know both my Father and Mother worked hard and did the best they could for us during the depression years because money was extremely tight and hard to come-by.

I recall that one day Mother took me to the Perkins Department Store in Troutdale where I saw a pocket book that I wanted. I had a dime and I needed the pocketbook to keep the dime in, but if I spent my dime I no longer needed the pocket book. At an early age this was hard for me to figure out.

HYGIENE

For many years, a toothbrush and tooth paste were out of the question so Mother taught us how to make our own toothbrush. We were instructed to take a small birch tree branch and then chew the end of it until it became frayed. Then using soda or salt we could brush and scrub our teeth.

Soap for bathing was another issue. When a hog was killed Mother would take all the non-edible parts of the hog like the stomach, intestines, ears, etc., and make soap. To these entrails she would add some Red Devil Lye and would cook the mixture until all parts were dissolved. When the mixture had boiled-down it became thick and then set aside to cool. This soap known as lye soap was good for the washing and cleaning of about anything.

ENTERTAINMENT ON THE FARM

As children our entertainment consisted mostly of playing games like hide-and-seek, checkers and base-ball if we could rally enough of the neighbor's kids and kinfolks. When it snowed we would go sledding on a homemade sled[8]. The rider sat on the main part of the sled and placed his or her feet on the back of the guide-sled. In this manner you could guide the sled in the direction you wanted to go by turning it right or left with your feet. Lastly a rope was tied to the front sled for ease in pulling it back to the top of the hill.

DAILY SKILLS

I have both my Father and Mother to thank for instilling in me a good work ethic and providing me with the necessary skills to survive in a poverty stricken farming environment. My Father was mostly focused on mechanical, farming and hunting endeavors. By the time I was fifteen years old my father had taught me to rebuild a wagon wheel, weld a steel wagon tire by building a small fire from wood chips to heat the tire red hot and using a hammer to pound it, draw a steel tire onto a wooden wheel by heating it to the correct temperature with wood chips to make it expand then pour water on it after it was installed to make it shrink. My Father also taught me other mechanical skills: how to make and install a wagon axle, make a wagon bed, build a horse sled for hauling wood, plow with a team of horses, mow hay, rake and stack hay, feed a thrashing machine, cut and shuck corn, strip and cut cane to make molasses, build a furnace out of stone and mud to make molasses, construct a building, paint, and make a wheelbarrow.

My Mother taught us many housekeeping skills: how to use a needle and thread to do clothing repair and make alterations; how to gather, prepare and cook food, and how to properly clean the house and do laundry. The Lovelace children of Troutdale all moved into adulthood competent with many daily skills and the confidence they could succeed in life because of the foundation given us by two devoted parents.

FASCINATION WITH ENGINE POWERED EQUIPMENT

As a boy I was always looking to accomplish my work the easiest way possible. I recall at times I would build smaller wagons to accomplish some task but when I finished and loaded them, they were always too heavy to move the load. There had to be a better way so I thought and conceived of how I might attach a small gasoline engine to a wagon to move it more efficiently. I bought an engine from Willie Barker and my first attempt was to try to fit the engine to a bicycle, however, I was never able to make that work. So much for the idea of motorized wagons, but even today I'm still fascinated with motors and powered vehicles.

HUNTING & TRAPPING

Early in life I learned the value of a dollar and of a need to become self-sufficient. About ten years of age I began hunting wild rabbits and squirrels with a twelve-gauge shot gun or twenty-two caliber rifle. I also set rabbit traps and sold the rabbits to the local country store. A big rabbit would bring twenty-five cents and a small one, fifteen cents. Of course one could hunt opossums and skunks whose hides would bring about thirty-five cents if the pelts were good and had not been cut while skinning. My father saw to it that I visited the traps every day so as not to mistreat and punish the animals. I usually visited the traps before I went to school, often before daylight. On one occasion I caught a skunk in a rabbit trap. I got hold of his tail, pulled it out and carried it to the house. My father told me to put a stick of wood across its neck and pull it by the hind legs and break its neck so as not to bruise the hide. This I did while he laughed behind my back. What do you think I got right in the face the first time I pulled on its hind legs? You guessed it, a good shot of skunk scent. I turned it loose and it started to run so I picked up a stick of wood to throw at it and when I threw it I hooked my toe over a board and fell right under it and it let me have it again. Two shots right in the face was enough for any young hunter so I let him go. My father, who was still laughing knocked the skunk in the head and it immediately passed away.

My friend Elden and I often went opossum hunting at night. On one occasion the dogs chased a skunk into a hole. It was too big for the hole and could not get all the way in. We could see his rear end. We always carried a gun with us on these trips. Elden shined a flashlight over the gun sights and I shot and killed the skunk without making a hole in the hide. Guess where I hit it? You are right, especially when he was approached from behind. I received prime payment for that skunk because the shot exited his head area and no hole was made in the hide.

VISITING NEIGHBORS

Occasionally my father and I would ride our horse bareback to Mr. and Mrs. Pruitt's home on Comers

Creek, a distance of about two and one-half miles. We would generally stay at the Pruitt's for lunch and then ride back home. The ride to and from their home was the most fun.

OUR HORSE

It seems we always had one old horse. The first horse that I remember was named Jim. Well old Jim was an ornery old horse but very smart. He could use his nose to open almost any of the gates and the barn doors. Special latches had to be installed to keep him where he was supposed to stay. If you were riding him and you placed your hand behind you on the top of his hips you could expect to be bucked off. I suppose that was a signal for him to buck. Someone said that he was once a show horse and was trained to buck. My father was very kind to Jim as he was to all animals. He never liked lending Jim out to work. However, if he did he would take Jim and personally handle him or at least stay with him all day to see that he was treated right. On this one occasion he lent him to a farmer to do some plowing and did not go with him. Jim was worked hard all day and fed dry feed for his noon meal and was not given any water all day. A few days after lending Jim out he died. My father performed an autopsy on Jim. He found an impacted stomach. Dry food without water impacted Jim's stomach and caused inflammation in the stomach lining. This was a terrible thing to happen to an animal. Jim's passing was an emotional loss for our family because Jim was like one of the family. Also, we would have to replace Jim soon for without a horse doing the heavy work of plowing, towing and lifting our farm would not survive. I believe Jim was about twenty years old when he died.

MY COUSIN'S VISIT

On one occasion a distant cousin came to spend the night and of course we didn't have an extra bed so he had to sleep with my grandfather. It was raining hard that night so what better time for him to have a nightmare? He was sleeping in bed next to the wall behind my grandfather, when about 12 o'clock that night he kicked my grandfather out of bed then dived through a twelve-pane window taking the whole bottom half of the window with him. He ran around the house three or four times hollering "Hello Mr. Britches, Britches, Britches." Then all was silent and my cousin disappeared. My father became very concerned and went to my half-sister's house and awoke her husband, Bruce Walton. They both took a lantern and tracked him through the mud out through a field and down over a road bank that was about twelve feet high and headed for Troutdale. After walking a little over a mile they met a barefoot man and called out and asked if it was he and he responded that it was. My cousin explained that he had run into a mud hole and woke up. This did not make sense after traveling over a mile in a hard rain but what nightmare makes sense? He had borrowed a pair of pants from

George Henderson, the town blacksmith, and was on his way back. He only had on his long handle under-wear when he left. It was about two A.M. when all this was over. Needless to say no one got back to sleep that night. My cousin was embarrassed beyond comprehension and offered to pay for the window. I thought it all was funny. I enjoyed the excitement!

DISCIPLINE

The mention of corn reminds me of the time that my father was plowing corn and at one end of the field the corn was really tall for the time of year. For some reason only a child could explain, I borrowed his pocket knife and while he plowed to the other end of the field, I cut all of the large corn. I don't remember if he spanked me or not but I will remember the incident for as long as I live.

BEGINNING SCHOOL

I was about seven years old when I started school. The first school that I attended was in an old country church that was used for a school house during the week. It was called the Comers Creek Elementary School. It had one room and all the grades were together. One teacher taught all the grades. We had no rest rooms or inside plumbing, only outside privies. Our drinking water was carried from a nearby spring at a neighbor's house. We used a two gallon-galvanized bucket for a water bucket. There was a large dipper for everyone to drink from.

My sister, Margaret and I walked about two miles to school and in the winter time it was so cold on some days that we tied handkerchiefs over our mouth and nose to keep out the cold. Many days it would get as low as fifteen below zero in the western part of Grayson County. Many times the handkerchief would freeze. Margaret always looked after me. Later in life when she went to work she would give me money when I needed it. I remember sometimes in the summertime my friend, Elden Mabe, Margaret, and I would take a short cut through a pasture field on our way home from school. On one occasion we found a pack of Beechnut Chewing tobacco and of course we had to try it out. Elden chewed a little too much and got sick. Not knowing the danger he was in, we left him sick and vomiting in the pasture field where there was a bad bull. The bull didn't find him and he later made it home okay. He was lucky.

The teachers were assigned by the school board and sent to the location. Room and board was acquired by the teacher in a local residence, usually a family by the name of King. One day the teacher went home with Margaret and me. I don't recall if she spent the night. I do remember that my father was telling her about the time that he got his thumb injured in the cane mill. As it happened the cogs on the rollers caught his thumb and cut it off just behind the thumb nail but it did not break the bone. A little bone was protruding out of the flesh. He took the end that was cut off and put it back on and bound it up with a piece of white cloth. While he was telling the teacher about it she almost fainted and my mother had to let her smell some ammonia to revive her. His thumb healed back and I don't think he ever went to the doctor.

SCHOOL CONSOLIDATION

The school board closed the school at Comers Creek and consolidated it with the Troutdale school about the time I started the third grade. The Troutdale High School and Elementary School were something to behold. After the one room school at Comers Creek, this was a mansion. It had four teachers and four rooms to include the High School. One room had the first, second and third grades, in the next room was the fourth and fifth grade, the next room held the sixth and seventh grade, and the last room was for the eighth, ninth, tenth and eleventh grade.

There were only eleven grades in high school in those years.

The second floor of the new school building had an auditorium with a stage, curtains and piano. I think back on this space and remember all the fun things in this auditorium like the Christmas plays, parties and other gatherings. Many traveling entertainers made appearances there including "The Roy Rogers and Dale Evans Show". The second floor also served as our cafeteria with a kitchen and a place for mischief. One day, two leading high school students (a young man and young lady) were caught behind the piano doing what young people like to do.

Even with a much better facility there was still no inside plumbing, so we continued hauling water in buckets, sharing a water dipper and using outside privies. Some years later restrooms were constructed on one side of the dirt basement floor.

SCHOOL PRANKS

The Federal Government had set up sewing rooms in the town during the great depression to give the women jobs. One such sewing room was in an old warehouse on my way home from school. It had only one entrance and exit door near the sidewalk. On that door was a latch that could be closed and locked. One day Elden Mabe and I, on the spur of the moment, decided to lock them up. I went first and folded the latch over the staple and he came along behind me and dropped a stick in it. Another student came along behind us in about five minutes and saw the women trying to get out. She took the stick from the latch and let them out. Someone recognized us and told the school principal, Mr. Andrews, they had been locked up for hours and that some of the women had missed their ride home. We knew that we would be corrected. On Friday our teachers told us that the principal wanted us to stay after school. He came in and had a good heart to heart talk with us and then sent us out to get a switch to use on us with the instructions not to bring back a twig. We got a good two-handed switch about five feet long and took it to him. He gave us three good hits each on the legs with both hands and told us he had to do something to us because we had interfered with a government project. I stood with my pant legs loose so I didn't feel anything. When he got to Elden, he made him put his hands over his head which in turn tightened his pants against his legs. He got three large red welts on each leg and I got none. When I told my father about the incident, he asked me if I had learned anything from it. Ha!

This same building had a roof that came within about three feet off the ground at the back. One could easily get on the roof at that point. One Halloween a friend of mine and I borrowed a bucket from our friend's house (Margaret Long) and filled it with water and climbed on the roof and waited for someone to come by. As it turned out this mean old lady that lived down the street came walking by. Just at the right time I poured about half of the water on her head. She didn't say a word but continued on to the store. On her way back she walked right under us again and I poured the rest of the water on her. Again she said nothing but continued on to her house. When she came out again she had a big long-barreled pistol. We immediately got off the roof and ran!

One Halloween the older students turned the women's privy upside down after school was dismissed. Needless to say that the next day, school was dismissed early and the students were told to undo their prank. No punishment was given them. The next morning everything was back in its place.

SKIPPING SCHOOL

The best way to be sent home from school without punishment was: to get close to a skunk and get his scent on you then change all your clothes except your belt. When the teacher smelled the skunk scent, she would send you home.

SCHOOL PLAYS

It was on the school stage that I became fond of school plays and made many appearances. One play that we put on at Thanksgiving comes to mind. I was told to dress a turkey in the play. It was my job to go out one of the doors and return with a dress on a turkey. Of course this was a play on "turkey dress-ing" with a hilarious punch-line! This was humor in the 1930s.

TEACHERS & DISCIPLINE

I had some really good teachers. One stands out above all the others. Her name was Miss Alma Wil-liams Andrews. She was very strict and made us get our lessons well. Miss Andrews frequently used spanking as discipline. She would turn you over a desk in the presence of the students and give you a spanking if she thought it was necessary. While this behavior today would probably be called abuse, this old-time discipline I believe helped to turn-out better students during this time. As a youngster I needed all the help I could get and Miss Andrews obliged me with lots of character building and encouragement. Another excellent teacher was Miss Lois Phipps who also encouraged and helped her students to gain self-confidence and to take initiative in their studies.

EATING AT SCHOOL

Not having much to make sandwiches from, I remember sometimes taking cold, leftover buck-wheat pancakes to school for lunch. They were not very appetizing, but they were filling and served their purpose when you were hungry.

NOTICING GIRLS AT SCHOOL

Taking notice of girls began for me at about eleven years old. I remember on one occasion two of my female classmates came to our house (Virginia Lantz and Viona Blevins). I was so embarrassed because you see being so poor we could not buy wall paper so our house was papered from old Montgomery Ward catalog pages (not very attractive). After their visit I walked the girls the mile long journey back to Troutdale and was able to counter my embarrassment in treating them to a bag of store-bought candy.

SCHOOL SPORTS

Times were simpler in the 1930s and I tried most everything at school. I joined and played on the Troutdale school basketball team. Not much to tell about my accomplishments as a five-foot, three-inch player except it was fun!

I also played on the school baseball team with my primary position as shortstop. Occasionally I was called to play other positions like pitching and catching. I did not like the catcher position because every time the batter would swing I shut my eyes! Sometimes the batter would hit the ball and sometimes the ball would hit me! I went home many evenings with a bruised or dislocated finger from the batter missing the ball. I would not tell my father of the baseball injuries because chores at home held a higher importance than just about anything else. I simply was too afraid to experience the wrath of Mr. Cary Robert Lovelace for allowing such a thing to happen.

The school had no athletic equipment except what the principal bought out of his own pocket. We had only two baseballs to practice with and when the cover was ripped I would take it home and sew it back. To do this I had to soak the leather cover in warm water and sew it before it dried out with two needles using a cotton thread that had been waxed

with beeswax. The leather would stretch when wet
and when it dried it would shrink and be very tight
on the ball. If a basket ball seam ripped, I would take
it home, turn it inside out and sew it. If the bladder
burst, I would patch it too.

FIGHTING AT SCHOOL

Moving to the new school helped me grow a big chip
on my shoulder. As a young man I had somewhat of a
Napoleon complex in that I was short, overly aggres-
sive and looking for a fight. To prove my toughness
early-on in school I decided to take a stand to fight
bullies and name-callers. I simply would not let them
push me around nor in anyway intimidate me into
submission to their demands. Generally through no
fault of my own I was in a fight almost every week.
My fuse was short and the smallest of insults like
someone calling me a liar or teasing me about my
ragged clothes or my size was enough to stir-up my

anger. While in school I was generally smaller than most opponents weighing only about 115 pounds. Most fights would occur in the afternoon just after school. My favorite fist fight was to knock my opponent down, sit straddle on his body and hit him in the nose until it bled which would scare him good. On occasion I was whipped. I remember a fight once with a redheaded boy. The fight ended-up covering about two city blocks. I guess the fight was a draw since neither of us knocked the other down. Surprisingly I never had a teacher caution me about fighting nor did my father ever question my bumps, bruises, or cuts and neither did I ever tell him.

NO PTA IN THE 1930S

During my school years there was no Parent Teacher Association (PTA). My father believed that teachers held very honorable and responsible jobs, but should be made accountable in how they handled their classrooms. Thus he took it upon himself to oversee their work and guidance especially of those teachers who taught his children. He had no problem confronting the teachers and the school when he believed things were handled improperly. After dealing with my father for a while the school seemed to become more fearful of him than the school board.

SCHOOL HEADACHES & SCHOOL JOB

I began to have tremendous headaches during my latter school years. They were so severe that I would get sick on my stomach and vomit until there was nothing but green phlegm coming out. A doctor was out of the question so my father would press on my temples with his thumbs for a long period of time to help reduce the pain. I suppose it was caused from stress or something I had eaten. The most pressing issue in my young life was peer pressure at school.

We were poor and decent clothing for the Lovelace kids to fit-in was out of the question.

I obtained a job at school with the help of my teacher, Miss Alma Williams. The work required that I come to the school early in the morning and build a fire in each of the large pot-bellied coal stoves. Each of the four stoves stood in one corner of each classroom. The rooms had to be warm by the time the teachers and students arrived. The second part of my job was to sweep the floors. The floors were treated with used motor oil to keep down the dust. The job paid fifteen dollars per month while school was in session. Fifteen dollars was the most money I had ever had or made and enabled me to buy new school pants and shirts. After my first pay day I was no longer called the "rag boy" so I held on to this job for quite some time. Seems this is when my severe headaches, upset stomach and vomiting ceased. Looking back, Miss Alma Williams was a thoughtful teacher helping her students any way she could.

MISSING SCHOOL & REGRETS

I can't approximate how many days of school I missed, only that I didn't make it to school as often as I could or should have. After all I was a farming kid where work and chores took priority over school attendance and school work. School is one of the necessities that I wish I would have taken more seriously and exerted more effort early in my life.

LEAVING SCHOOL

At fifteen and after much discussion and criticism I left school for work. After all I had finished the sixth grade. I had many older friends in the community that encouraged me to stay in school but you know how that is, I knew more than they did. I went to Marion and applied for a job at the Lincoln Furniture factory. The foreman took one look at me and said that I was not old enough. I told him that I was

eighteen and he said you don't even have a beard.
Two weeks later I grew a beard and went back but
he would not give me a job. After a while I managed
to get a job at Harwood Mfg. Co., a garment mill.
The superintendent gave me a job to look after
their victory garden. By this time the United States
had been in World War II about two years, and
most companies of any size had a Victory Garden
to signify patriotism and support the war effort. I
worked so hard that I kept running out of things to
do so they gave me a job inside the factory spread-
ing cloth on tables for the cutters. I now was called
a spreader. I was now in the money. I was making
seventeen dollars and fifty cents a week and could
go to the movies. I rode the work bus from Troutdale which was about eighteen miles. It cost about
six dollars a week so I had money left over after all
expenses. I worked at Harwood from July 1943 until
January 1944. My reason for leaving Harwood was
that Uncle Sam pointed his finger at me and said "I
want you!"

WAR RATIONING

During the war years we could only get about five pounds of sugar each month and other necessities because everything was rationed. An empty tube of toothpaste had to be turned in to get another tube. Gasoline stamps were issued only for travel to and from work. If you were caught traveling by car to town to see a movie you would be fined ten dollars. Automobile tires were also rationed. If a tire had a hole in it the bead could be cut off an old tire and installed over the other old tire covering the hole. The vehicle would then be drivable again. This worked rather well for driving slow except if you stopped too quickly the inner tire would slide inside the outer tire and could potentially catch fire.

GETTING MY
DRIVER'S LICENSE

A friend of mine, Billy Joe Handy and I hitch hiked twenty five miles to Independence, VA to get our driver's license. Billy Joe told me that a friend of his was there and we could use his car. He didn't explain why we could not have ridden down with him. Anyway when we got to town Billy Joe walked up and down the street until he found a car with the ignition keys in the switch. He said this is the one, so with the official issuing the permit we each drove around the court house and parked. To this day I don't know whose car we used and I am sure that they didn't know we had used it either. We both got our license that day. The cost was fifty cents each. Before leaving Independence we got a little more practice by driving the car around the courthouse and re-parking. We returned to Troutdale by hitch-hiking but now with our driver's license in-hand.

WALKING TO VISIT GIRLS
& LOCAL YAHOOS

When I was about sixteen three friends of mine, Warren Dempsey, Carl Campbell and Robert Barker walked about four miles to church at Grant, VA just to see the girls. After church at night we would walk the girls home and then walk back to Trout-dale. There was a beautiful girl, Charlsey Hall, that I was walking home one night when one of the local yahoos about six feet tall told me that I should go back. I told him that I had promised Charlsey that I would walk her home and that is what I was going to do. What I did not know was that two of my friends had sensed trouble and had followed close behind. This big fellow went back to talk to them and Warren told him he had two choices, to shut up or turkey trot for him and pulled out a thirty-eight special pistol. That was the end of that. I found out later that Charlsey was only thirteen and that she was too young for me so I didn't see her anymore.

She sent word by my sister for me to come and see her after the war but to this day I have not seen her. I dated another fine Christian girl in the area, Sarah Campbell, for some time after that.

Robert Barker and I sometimes would walk to Sherwood Anderson's (the novel writer's) cabin on Ripshin Creek where there was a resort nearby that the Marion College girls would spend some time each summer. We did not date any of them but we had fun just going there, if nothing more than harassing the chaperons. Once on this trip I sprained my ankle and walked about four miles on it. Needless to say I had a 'shoe full' the next day. I often spent the night in Robert Barker's home. His father, Nicholas, was a fine man and a good friend of my father. I always felt welcome there.

CHAPTER 3

WORLD WAR II

ARMY INDUCTION

At the age of eighteen weighing only 118 pounds I joined Uncle Sam's US Army. An appendectomy provided a 30 day temporary stay from military service, but soon after I recovered and was on my way to becoming a soldier. Up until the US declared war most people including myself were hoping that Hitler was only a "howling blow-hard" who would soon be stopped by the great European powers. Most thought, at best, US involvement would only be a minor skirmish. Nevertheless, war became a reality on December 7, 1941, when the Japanese bombed Pear Harbor and the US declared war.

THE MILITARY PHYSICAL

My medical examination took place on January 26, 1944 at the induction station in Abingdon, VA. I did not understand all the different examinations that I was given at that time. One of the stations was in a large room with only two chairs in the middle of the floor. There was an elderly man with white hair and a white goatee sitting in one of the chairs. He invited me to sit down facing him and started to ask me questions. In the meantime he tapped me on the knee with his little rubber hammer to check my reflexes. His questions and my answers were:

Do you like girls?
My answer: Some I do and some I don't.

Robert becomes Company Clerk

Do the girls like you?
My answer: Some do and some don't.

Do you have enough spending money?
My answer: No.

I found out later that he was a Psychiatrist. My answers must have been acceptable because I passed the examination. One of the tests was to see if you were color-blind. I knew about the test so I played off color-blind. If I was color-blind, they would not take me into the navy. After I had completed all the physical exams and was considered fit for the service, I was sent before a selection board of three officers, one officer for the Navy, Air Force and Army. The Naval officer said it was his turn so he picked me for the Navy. He looked at my exam papers and noted that I was color-blind and passed me onto the Army officer which is what I wanted.

BASIC TRAINING

Infantry basic training which lasted seventeen weeks was hard, fair and fun. The uniform was nice but incomplete without the canvas lace-up leggings. The platoon Sergeant allowed a ten minute break each hour which many of the men used to smoke. During the break it was soon discovered that a lit cigarette when held against a buddy's flammable legging string could prove a great source of entertainment. The string would burn very slowly and when the break was over and we were called back into formation his legging would fall off. This would cause him a source of personal stress but humor for those observing. Graduation from boot camp ended with a twenty-five-mile march from the bivouac area back to camp. After all the training the march seemed a breeze and I was proud that I made it in good time.

DEPLOYMENT

Guarding German POWs

As a private my basic pay to start was fifty dollars per month. I reported for duty on February 16, 1944 to Fort George G. Meade, MD. Since I was under nineteen at that time a government regulation kept me from combat. I begged to go fight in Europe; however, I was told there were too many 18 year olds dying and a regulation excluded me from combat. After three or four days at Fort Meade I was assigned and sent to guard German POWs at Drew Field Army Base in Blanding, FL. I was one of about sixty men sent to guard three hundred prisoners at the camp. The camp was located adjacent to the Rocky Point Golf Course clubhouse jut off Memorial Highway near Tampa, FL.

Our POWs were to work on the Air Base. This worked out very well although we did not have enough guards for this many prisoners. I have guarded eighty POWs on railroad work spread out for a mile with sixteen rounds of ammunition. Many times I have guarded prisoners at work for eight hours and then pulled four hours of tower guard duty that night. Prisoners seemed to like the treatment they received and were not interested in going anyplace. I never lost a prisoner. The government paid them ten cents an hour for their work. Since they were limited as to where they could spend their earnings many saved thousands of dollars while in the US.

Military Housing

Our housing at the base was in the Women's Auxiliary Corps (WAC) barracks. These accommodations were nicer than the men's in that they were equipped with built-in ironing boards, clothes cabinets, and indoor latrines with stalls. Better even than the accommodations was the adjoining 18 hole golf course. The golf course was hardly used by civilians

POW Camp in Florida

Soldiers at the Chapel after Sunday Church

and under-managed by the Air Force but was in just enough shape for us to play on.

Pay Raises and Other Income

After being at the base for about a year I was promoted to Corporal and my pay was increased to $60 per month. Nonetheless, coming from a family of poverty in Grayson County I was continually thinking of how I might earn extra income. I presented an idea to my company commander that if he could obtain a barber chair that I would install it in the barracks washroom and cut the men's hair for 35 cents per head. This rate matched the Post Exchange's rate plus it would free-up time when waiting in line and lessen the walk to and from the Exchange. I felt I had all the experience necessary for a military barber in that I had cut my brothers' hair at least four or five times in the past. To earn even more income I began to wash, starch and iron cotton-khaki uniforms for fifty cents; sell brass-polish for seventy-five cents, and take another's guard duty for $2 per night. I also went to base typing school during the evening and was subsequently awarded by the base commander the job of Company Clerk. I did make a "tiny" mistake once on this job. I had read where one Army regulation awarded three days leave at Christmas for all soldiers and so I told the commander about the regulation. I also suggested he might consider giving all married men leave for Christmas and the non-married men leave at New Year's. He agreed so I made and distributed the passes. The mistake that I made was in overlooking the sentence that qualified the regulation to "only during peace-time". However, since the commander had already granted the leave he let them all go. He never said anything to me about the mistake.

Army Healthcare

My first great challenge in the Army was with a young second lieutenant dentist. When he saw me he seemed upset about the condition of my teeth which needed five fillings. I was in the chair about three hours while he drilled and complained about my teeth. In those days Novocain was not in use. The anxiety and confrontation came when he drilled deep and began to hit nerves. He would squirt cold water in the cavity then dry it out with cold air. He drilled so long that the drill became hot (the old belt driven types) and burned my tongue. One time he let the drill slip off the tooth and cut the inside of my jaw. When he started to fill the tooth, he dropped the filling in my eye. After a while I began to move around then he tried to hold me and drill more. I didn't know you were not supposed to talk back to an officer. I was about to hit him when he decided to stop drilling for a while. This was the longest time that I have ever spent in a dentist chair. Another dentist months later, removed most of the fillings the lieutenant had put in and did everything correctly and he did not hurt me in the process. At the age of

97, I am proud to say that my teeth are strong with some fillings and a bridge or two.

FUN WITH MILITARY BUDDIES & FRIENDS

Driving and Shooting Skills

My best buddy was Jadie Williams who was always doing crazy stuff. On one occasion a prisoner was poking fun at Americans for not being able to shoot well. My friend turned and shot a sea gull's head off about one hundred yards away. It was pure luck but the prisoner didn't tease him anymore.

Adjacent to the golf course was a wooded area where Jadie taught me how to drive a government vehicle called a carryall. He would intentionally get a carryall stuck in the marsh and let me get it out. After a period of time the Air Force told us not to do this anymore and they repaired the damage. I received enough experience to get a military license and eventually a Florida state license.

Bane Wright and his Sister

A young man named Bane Wright from Marion, VA, and I were both inducted at the same time but his health was poor so he was sent home before finishing basic training. I visited him on military leave and met his sister, Ester. I dated Ester for a while on military leaves and wrote her, but by the time I was discharged she had moved-on and had obtained work at Aberdeen Proving Ground in MD.

THE LOST SHEEP

Jadie Williams and I were on the air base and saw a sheep grazing so we put it in the jeep and took it back to the Prisoner of War camp. We went right through the Military Police at the gate without them questioning why we had a sheep in the jeep. We were trying to put it in Captain Drewry's (the Company Commander's) hut when he walked up and caught us. He asked us what we were doing and we told him we were putting a sheep in his quarters. He just laughed and went on. After a week or so the hospital put out a bulletin for the sheep. How were we to know it was one of their experimental research sheep at the hospital? We called and informed them where the sheep was and they came and got it.

Once Jadie Williams and I wanted to go to town but we didn't have transportation so we borrowed an old 1935 ford coupe from a soldier friend from Arkansas (Pvt. Sutton). He told us the brakes were not very good. I had gotten a Florida drivers license since Jadie had trained me how to drive on the dirt roads around the golf course. I was driving as we came upon a four-lane highway. I had not checked the brakes so when I stepped on them there wasn't any brakes at all. We went right through the intersection but did not hit anyone. We drove around town that night without any brakes. We just geared it down when we wanted to stop. This was an experience since Tampa, Florida was a city of about 90 thousand at that time. We had a lot of fun.

"RIDEM COWBOY"

One day a farmer's horse got out and was grazing next to our barracks. We had a guy from Indiana that bragged about how well he could ride. He mounted the horse and apparently the horse did not like it so the horse got his pant leg in his mouth and pulled him off. We called a radio station and had a song played for him "Ridem Cowboy." We had to hold him down and make him listen to it.

THE EISENHOWER JACKET
& THE ROSEN GIRLS

While I was guarding prisoners at the base many of the enlisted men began wearing Eisenhower Jackets. We were allowed to modify our uniform coat to resemble the Eisenhower Jacket. I had a lot of pride in my uniform so the alteration had to look professional. An excellent tailor named Mrs. Rosen lived about a mile from the barracks so I sought her out to modify my coat. What I didn't know was Mrs. Rosen had three beautiful daughters named Dorothy, Betty and Gloria. Dorothy was 16, Betty 18 and Gloria 22 who was married. I met with Mrs. Rosen to drop-off the jacket and was invited back the next Sunday to attend church with them. My friend Jadie came along and we went to church with the Rosen family. I must say it was my first-time experience in that Jadie placed a dollar in the offering plate and took back 50 cents in change. I had never seen anyone make change out of an offering plate. One thing led to another and it wasn't long before Betty and I became good friends. Betty was a good Christian girl who neither drank nor smoked, nor had any other vices. Betty and I became very close and did most everything together for over a year. We went to football games, the movies, fishing, fairs, walks, playing golf and of course to church. Skating was another of our favorite places to go for entertainment. I was a good skater with excellent speed and was frequently being cautioned to slow-down or get off the floor. Betty and I loved to go to the rink with Jadie because it always provided an opportunity to laugh at Jadie who could not skate a lick. No doubt the janitor work was lessened after Jadie polished the skating rink floor with his rear.

Mrs. Rosen was like a second mother who was constantly having me over to dinner. I returned the favor by driving her places in her old Plymouth. After pulling guard-duty all night, I once fell asleep while driving Mrs. Rosen and Betty to town. The car swerved left and I immediately woke-up. I heard Mrs. Rosen comment to someone later that Robert sure knows how to miss pot-holes. She never knew that I had fallen asleep!

WOMEN'S NYLON HOSE

During the war ladies' nylon hose was almost impossible to find. Once my captain heard there was someone selling nylons near the base and since there was a limit of two pair per buyer he came by our quarters and asked if I and another soldier would go with him and get the extra hose for his wife. The captain came and woke us around 3 A.M. to get a jump on the other buyers. When arriving where the nylons were being sold, there was already a line a tenth of a mile long. We discovered that some soldiers had been waiting there all night! However, we were able to purchase the nylons, but our in-line wait time was about five hours. We sure hoped his wife appreciated those nylons and our loss of sleep.

THE END OF WORLD WAR II

The war officially ended with the surrender of the
Japanese on September 2, 1945; however, my return
home would not occur until early 1946. Betty Rosen
and I had become close and she became extremely
upset when she found out that I was preparing to
leave Florida. Just prior to the end of the war I was
transferred to a German prisoner of war camp in
Daytona Beach but I continued to go see Betty in
Tampa. I knew Betty really liked me because once
when she had to work all night in her job as a tele-
graph operator she became really upset with me
when I took her sister Dorothy to a football game.
When the war ended I was transferred to Fort Mead,
MD, where I was discharged on May 9, 1946. I really
cared for Betty but since I was out of a job, and had
no money and no place to stay, I wasn't ready to go
back to Florida. I wrote Betty for awhile after I came
home then stopped.

Robert demonstrating plowing skills

Homeplace barn with father

CHAPTER 4

AFTER THE WAR

RECONNECTING WITH ESTER WRIGHT

Upon being discharged I had hoped to reconnect with Ester Wright, but found that she had left Troutdale and was working at Aberdeen Proving Ground in MD. Since I did not have a car I talked my cousin Thelma Osborne, who had a car, and my sister Margaret into going to a place called Street, MD to visit my half-sister Rachel. My ulterior motive was of course to see Ester. It was a great visit but I was

only able to visit Ester this one time and never had
the opportunity to see her again.

KEEPING BUSY WITH
TROUTDALE HOUSE REPAIRS

By 1946 the Troutdale farmhouse needed painting and the picket fence had rotted down. First, the
house was painted with 10 gallons of paint. Second,
a new picket fence was made and installed. A friend
of mine, Kent Testerman and I cut pine trees in the
mountain with a cross cut saw and skidded the logs
out with a horse to the road where they could be
hauled to a sawmill and cut into lumber to rebuild
the fence. The lumber was rough sawed at the saw
mill and delivered without being finished. I personally cut the lumber into pickets with a handsaw and
dressed them by hand with a wood plane. It took
more than thirteen hundred pickets to go around the
yard (435 ft) and one hundred and ten two-by-fours
for the fence rails. There were 56 posts which I cut

from locust trees and installed. So you see it took quite awhile to get this done. I did not quite finish the fence so I had my brother Donald to finish it.

MY FIRST CAR

I learned to drive while stationed in Florida where I became used to driving military vehicles and other people's cars. So upon discharge and arrival back to Troutdale, I began looking for a car. My first car purchased was in Bristol, TN. I gave $300 for a 1935 V-8 Ford with sixty-five horsepower. I don't know how many total miles the car had been driven, but I soon discovered the car's secret on my way back to Troutdale: it was worn-out! I had to use low-gear to climb even the little hills. I kept the car two weeks and took it back to the seller who offered $200 to buy it back. I regretted the thought of a $100 loss. In those days $100 was a lot of money. Since I felt I had little choice I took the deal and cut my losses.

JOINING THE ARMY RESERVE

The job market was extremely tight in 1946 so to stay occupied I joined the Army Reserve. I was first assigned to Battery B, 905th Glider Battalion, Field Artillery Bn. Headquarters 2nd US Army in Wytheville, VA. Joining the Reserve in 1946 unfortunately afforded no pay, no travel stipend and no uniform. However, the spirit of patriotism was at an all-time high in serving and in having won the war, so I felt good about joining. I am drawing retirement for those years now.

SEARCHING FOR WORK

A friend of mine Bud Testerman and I hitch hiked to Dover, New Jersey and got a job in a fiber mill. For some reason I did not like this job so after two weeks we quit and hitch hiked to Bluefield, WV and was going to work in the coal mines. I took one look at the mine entrance and that was enough for me!

I went back to Marion, VA and returned to work at the Harwood Manufacturing Company. I bought a 1940 Chevrolet from one of the employees while there. After a short time I became dissatisfied and left this employment. I got a job in the Marion Drug Store as a lunch counter manager trainee. After about six months the manager quit and I became manager with ten employees making one hundred and fifty dollars a month plus five percent of all gross sales over one hundred dollars each day which only amounted to five to ten dollars a month.

DATING & MARRIAGE

I was dating Gay Harrington that worked at another drug store up the street at the time. Gay and I didn't see each other as often as she would like because of the hours that we worked. She met someone else and decided she liked him more than me so we parted

Janice, my beloved, in 1948

— (Greear Photo)

RECENT BRIDE — Miss Janice Eva Buchanan, daughter of Mr. and Mrs. W. C. Buchanan of Sugar Grove, became the bride of Robert Lovelace, Jr., son of Mr. and Mrs. Robert Lovelace of Trout Dale. The double ring ceremony was performed Sunday, Sept. 14, at 10 o'clock at the home of Rev. W. H. Carter.

The bride wore an ice blue street-length dress with black accessories and a corsage of red rosebuds.

The couple left immediately for a short southern tour after which they will make their home in Marion where both are employed.

Janice and Robert's wedding announcement 1947

ways. One day this beautiful girl came into the drug store and sat down in a booth to have lunch. I had seen her in the store before and wanted to make her acquaintance. I made a remark to a bus driver friend of mine that I was going to marry that girl sitting over there. He said, who is she and I said, that I did not know but that I was going to find out. Well as luck goes I asked her for a date and she accepted. She worked in the office at the Brunswick plant in Marion. My friend, Kent Testerman, started dating her friend, Sally Betty Meek. We double dated a lot. Janice and I went to the tobacco warehouse in Abingdon, VA to dances where Tommy Dorsey's band played on some weekends. On one occasion my father wanted me to go to a farm near Tazewell, VA and pick up two pigs that he had bought. As it turned out, he wanted me to go on the same night that Kent and I had a date. We told the girls in advance but they were okay coming along to pick-up the pigs. We put the pigs in a burlap sack, put them in the trunk of the car and started back to Troutdale. The sack became untied and let them out and into the trunk. The pigs wanted out so much that by the time we reached home they had destroyed just about all the lining and wires in the trunk. They were making a mess of the trunk so as soon as we arrived at my father's farm I backed the car up to the pig pen, opened the trunk and let them out. This situation has given us many laughs over the years and has been a great story to share with friends.

While dating Janice, one Sunday morning I took a short cut on what was called the Hurricane road through the Jefferson National Forest to see her. This was a one lane gravel road aptly named as it was somewhat treacherous as it wound around the side of a mountain and down into a canyon. If one went over the side one would land in the tree tops. I wrecked about half way down the mountain. As luck would have it, I did not go over the bank. I just turned the old 1940 Chevrolet on its side and slid along the ditch. It stopped with the front-end out over the bank. With the wheel still spinning, I crawled out the passenger's side, which at this time was above me and started to walk out of the canyon. Someone came along and gave me a ride back to Troutdale. I had a friend to hook a chain to the car and turn it back on its wheels. Then I drove it to Marion for the necessary repairs. Unfortunately I missed my date with Janice, but was glad the car and I survived.

I soon afterward proposed to Janice and we were married three months later on September 14, 1947. Her mother was not happy about her getting married so young, (age 17), so we eloped and spent our first night at the foot of the Smokey Mountains in Sevierville, TN. While there we visited an army buddy of mine (Olin Catlett). From there we went to Pigeon Forge and Gatlinburg, TN. Then we drove up and over the Smokey Mountains to the Cherokee Indian Reservation in NC. After spending some time in Cherokee we proceeded on to visit Biltmore Estates in Asheville, NC. Then we headed back home and began our life together.

MANAGING TRAILWAYS BUS TERMINAL IN GALAX, VA

In May of 1948, I began working as Manager of the Trailways Bus Terminal in Galax, VA. The terminal included a restaurant and an Atlantic Oil Company service station. I soon learned the facility had many problems and personnel issues. The properties were owned by a doctor who I believed allowed himself to become too close to one of his employees. The employee reported to me and managed the restaurant operations. She disagreed with me (her boss) on almost everything. In one particular situation she was attempting to handle increases and decreases in restaurant supply cost by increasing and decreasing menu prices. This resulted in customer complaints and confusion because one never knew from one visit to the next if their food would cost the same, more, or less. I guess the real impasse came when she had the jukebox people remove a record that she didn't like but was well liked by the customers and bringing in lots of coins. I discovered what she had done and had the record placed back in the jukebox. We had a confrontation when she again had the record removed. I told her there was not enough room for both of us at the terminal and let her go. The owner was an older man with one blind eye and very little vision in the other eye. He was furious with me for firing his friend. We had a confrontation which at one point because of his anger, I thought he was going to use his cane on me. It was only at that time I understood how close he was to this employee.

WORKING & SETTLING IN THE ROANOKE VALLEY

Rather than make trouble I returned to Marion and resumed my old job of managing the lunch counter at the Marion Drug Store. My lunch counter job provided a paycheck but was far from a career. With a career in mind I began a job search as soon as we arrived back in Marion. In my job search Janice and I moved to Salem, VA in September 1948. Upon arrival in Salem we stayed with Janice's uncle and aunt, Jim and Ann Buchanan. After about two weeks I found employment and began working at the Rowe-Jordan Furniture factory. The job paid a whopping 45 cents per hour. I worked at Rowe-Jordan for only a few months then moved-on to the Veterans Hospital (VA) in Salem. I worked there as a Psychiatric Aide from December 1948 until August 1951. My pay at the VA was twenty-one hundred and seventy-five dollars ($2,175.00) per year. Working as a Psychiatric Aide I was given extensive training in psychology but really did not like the work. The VA continued to ask and pressure me to acquire more specialized training from the Mayo Clinic. After consideration I began looking for another line of work. Fortunately I was able to land a job at Burlington Industries in Salem. While employed at Burlington I mostly worked third shift which enabled me to continue educational endeavors. I worked at Burlington from September 1951 until May 1953 until being laid off. I found temporary work as a Shipping Clerk at Roanoke Iron and Bridge Company from May to September 1953, then from September 1953 to May 1955, I worked at Profitt's Esso Gas Station at which time I was called back to work at Burlington Industries. Upon returning to Burlington I worked six days a week and earned five-thousand two-hundred dollars ($5,200.00) per year as an operator of the hosiery knitting machine. This eighty-foot long machine had to be closely watched and maintained. The machine was capable of knitting thirty stockings at one time. Over an eight hour shift as an operator I would walk about 3 miles just watching over and circling the machine. During my second tour at Burlington I also had three part-time jobs in Roanoke as a mechanic on weekends at Bayse Esso Service Station, on Wednesday evenings at Jimmy Ellis' art business as a book-keeper, and on Thursday evenings at the Army Reserve. I continued employment with Burlington until the mill closed in November 1962. When Burlington closed I was also working Saturday nights for Bill Hale's Exxon on Plantation Road in Roanoke. Once while working there I remember a man walking into the station around 2 A.M. on a rainy night asking if he could just sit awhile in the office and dry-off a bit. I noticed each time a car would come in he would ask for a ride. Somewhere around 4 A.M. he got a ride and left with a man in a late model Chrysler. About 4:30 A.M. a State Trooper stopped in and asked if I had seen anyone fitting the stranger's description. I was shocked when I learned that the stranger was actually an escaped convict. I provided the trooper with a description of the man giving him a ride and the car they left in. I never heard whether or not he was caught.

My next full-time job was Durham Life Insurance Company. The job at Durham was interesting, but required long hours with some evening work for selling and collecting premium payments. I recall one stop in particular I made when attempting to make an insurance premium collection. The client was a lady with an eight-month old baby. She picked up the baby and sat down next to me on the couch so

I reached over to touch the baby's feet and made a remark that the baby looked like her husband. She agreed but commented that the baby was solid and firm like her. She then took my hand, placed it on her thigh and said: "you see what I mean?" I had stopped smoking about three months earlier; however, in noticing a pack of cigarettes and lighter on the table, I asked if I could possibly have one. She said yes so I lit the cigarette, excused myself and left the premises. The next time I went to collect at her house I knocked on the door and I heard her say "come-in". I stepped inside anxious and not knowing what to expect. She called to me and said that she was diapering the baby in the bedroom and that I should come on back. I told her I would just wait in the living room until she finished. When she came out of the bedroom she was apologetic saying that she decided to lapse the insurance policy. Her reason for letting the policy lapse was because her husband "was never going to die anyway". I excused myself and never went back but I did start smoking again. One of the other agents told a similar story. When he went to collect at a lady client's house she was standing on a chair hanging drapes. He claimed when she leaned over to step-down that one of her breasts popped-out of her dress. The agent left without making the collection and soon resigned.

One great benefit while working for Durham Insurance was that the District Manager would take us deep-sea fishing in Nags Head, NC. This trip was very enjoyable and a well-earned time away from our jobs. On one of our trips I made some "sop gravy" like my mother used to make. While I cooked, everyone made fun of the gravy making comments like "who could eat that stuff?" Then some of them tried the gravy and wanted me to make more at our next breakfast. I refused because of their making fun of the first batch.

After 13 years of service at Durham I had risen to an Agency Manager. I left Durham in April 1977, primarily because of the lengthy hours that the job required.

My final career move was with the US Government as a Civil Service employee. Finally I had a 40 hour work week. I began work for the Army Reserve in Martinsville, VA on 22 February 1977 for nine thousand three hundred and three dollars per year. I drove to work sixty miles each way every work day for six years. I was late to work only one day and that was because of an ice storm. My supervisor was Mr. Lawrence Taylor at the Salem, VA Army Reserve headquarters during the first six years that I worked in Martinsville. Unfortunately he died of a heart attack in 1982. Because of his death Mr. Lancaster took his job and I got Mr. Lancaster's job as Training officer, budget officer and assistant supervisor. Here I had more than a one million-dollar budget for the reserve's annual training plus about $178,000 that was to be used directly for the reserve unit such as travel and other individual pay. This promotion helped because I got a good raise plus I did not have to drive the 120 miles per day. I now had to drive only 9 miles one way per day to work.

I worked in Salem, VA headquarters until retirement from federal service in July 1993.

MY ARMY RESERVE CAREER

I rejoined the Army Reserve on April 1, 1956. I remained a member of the Army Reserve until September 9, 1985 and retired, (because of age restrictions) as a Sergeant Major with thirty-four years and nine months of military service of which more than twenty-nine years of reserve service was with the 2174th US Army Garrison and three years with a unit under the 2nd Army.

ARMY RESERVE STORY

Once we had a weekend meeting at Fort Picket, VA and the annual budget was being discussed. Several officers were present. Many of them were Lt. Colo-

THE UNITED STATES OF AMERICA

TO ALL WHO SHALL SEE THESE PRESENTS, GREETING: THIS IS TO CERTIFY THAT THE PRESIDENT
OF THE UNITED STATES OF AMERICA AUTHORIZED BY EXECUTIVE ORDER, 16 JANUARY 1969 HAS AWARDED

THE MERITORIOUS SERVICE MEDAL

TO   Sergeant Major ROBERT J. LOVELACE, United States Army Reserve

FOR   meritorious service during the period 8 February 1977 through 30 April 1984. During this
time Sergeant Major Lovelace distinguished himself as the Personnel Senior Sergeant, in-charge
of Detachment II, 217th United States Army Garrison, located at Martinsville, Virginia. His
dedication to duty, outstanding leadership and loyalty to the United States Army Reserve has
set the example for all to follow. Sergeant Major Lovelace's performance of duty has been far
superior to that of any other soldier. His ability to work and train his subordinates in all
aspect of military related work is unsurpassed. Sergeant Major Lovelace has brought an
exuberant amount of credit upon not only himself but the 217th United States Army Garrison,
the United States Army, and the United States Army Reserve.

GIVEN UNDER MY HAND IN THE CITY OF WASHINGTON
THIS   DAY OF MAY   19 84

JOHN P. HENDERSON, JR.

John O. Marsh, Jr.
SECRETARY OF THE ARMY

Meritorious Service Medal

DEPARTMENT OF THE ARMY

MR. ROBERT J. LOVELACE

IS PRESENTED THE

SUPERIOR CIVILIAN SERVICE AWARD

For Superior Service while serving as Staff Operations and Training Specialist
with the 217th U. S. Army Garrison, 80th Division (Training), Mr. Lovelace's
professionalism, dedication and attention to detail in the areas of training
and resource management contributed significantly to the Garrison's ability to
sustain a high level of operational readiness within its headquarters,
detachments and three independent companies as evidenced by multiple successful
overseas annual training periods and the mobilization and deployment of one
company during Operation Desert Shield/Storm, all bringing great credit upon
himself, the 80th Division and the entire Army Reserve Program.

MAX GUGGENHEIMER, JR.
Brigadier General, USAR
Commander, 80th Division (Training)

Superior Civilian Service Award (2nd highest award for civilians) nels and Colonels. The most important officer was General Guggenheimer from the 80th Division Training Headquarters. I have always been good at saying one thing, yet meaning another, but on this particular day all other faux pas of mine were surpassed. While I was presenting the budget General Guggenheimer asked me about one part of the budget handout. The budget handout was printed just before the meeting began so I told the General that the information he was asking about was on the printout "if it was not too complicated for him to understand". I should have chosen my words more carefully because what I meant to say was that I hoped he could understand the handout data the way it was presented in the format. All of the lesser ranked officers appeared very uneasy after my remark. I think they were waiting for the General to personally chew me out. General Guggenheimer said to me that he would talk with me concerning his question after the meeting. After the meeting he made no attempt to talk to me so while he was assembling his papers and preparing for departure I apologetically approached him. I told him that I had not meant my comment the way it came-out. He replied that he fully understood what I was trying to say that I had always been straight with him, and that I had never let him down before on anything. Needless to say I was very relieved!

RETIREMENT

Meritorious Service Medal and Superior Civilian Service Award

I retired from the Army Reserve on Orders # P-04-00197 dated 18 April 1985 effective 9 September 1985. My civil service retirement where I supported the 2174th US Army Garrison ended in July 1993. The following is a newspaper article covering service, awards and accomplishments during my forty-two years of government and military service. The article was written by 80th Division Special Writer, Jay Kincanon.

In January 1944, with World War II raging across the globe, Robert J. Lovelace joined the forces. Almost 40 years later, he decided to say "enough." Lovelace retired from the US Army Reserve.

"Life is a series of choices, and along the way I've made a few good ones-serving my country and my wife Janice" said Sgt. Maj. Lovelace during a recent retirement ceremony held in his honor. Lovelace received the distinguished Meritorious Service Medal for his dedicated service and uncompromising loyalty to the nation, the soldiers of the 2174th US Army Garrison and the US Army Reserve Program. Later the Superior Civilian Service Award was also awarded for significant contributions in the areas of training and resource management required for the Garrison's

*successful operational readiness, mobili-
zation and deployment. The award is the
second highest award that can be given
to a civilian employee.*

*During his 42 years of government
service, he spent 37 years in the 2174th
US Army Garrison, serving under every
commander the Garrison has had since
its formation. The Garrison is headquartered in Salem, VA and is part of the
80th Division which is headquartered in
Richmond, VA. There are a number of
soldiers from Radford and Montgomery
County areas. There are three reasons for
serving so long, Lovelace says, "One is
honor for country, second is monetary
compensation, and third is ambition."*

*Sgt. Maj. Lovelace's career is best
exemplified through his professional
dedication and his attention to planning and detail as noted in a 1987 80th*

Division audit report. "The 2174th has established an exemplary budget process whereby every staff section and subordinate command are directly involved..." Lovelace's efforts were the cornerstone of the entire budget process, from the early planning stages through the final accounting of funds expenditures at the end of the budget period. His oversight insured that scarce resources were conservatively applied so that unit mission and training requirement were funded as well as those requirements slated to occur during the budget period.

His initiative and persevering diligence insured the development and execution of sound training doctrines and plans that enabled the Garrison to provide technical and training assistance to three separate subordinate units which were tasked to perform vital roles in key mis-

sions during various periods of overseas training in Egypt, Honduras, Germany and Panama. The overall success which these units achieved can be directly attributed to Lovelace's perseverance in maintaining a high state of training readiness throughout the Garrison. The successful contribution which the 424th Transportation Company made to Operation Desert Shield/Storm upon it's mobilization and deployment to the theater of operations was unparalleled through his efforts in supervision and adherence to sound training doctrine.

Lovelace exemplifies the fact that Army reservists are indeed citizen soldiers dedicated to the service of their country and their fellow man. The dedication, diligence and attention to detail which were inherent characteristics of Lovelace's service, consistently earned him high marks from the 80th Division resource management and training staff personnel and brought great credit to himself, the 80th Division and the entire Reserve Program.

In addition to the above awards, Lovelace also received the following while on active duty in World War II and the Army Reserve: National Defense Service Medal, Good Conduct Medal, Army Achievement Medal, Army Commendation Medal, American Theater Ribbon, WWII Victory Ribbon, Army Service Ribbon, Meritorious Service Medal, six awards of Army Reserve Components Achievement Medal, and three Commanders Awards (one each from three different commanders).

Robert Lovelace served in the World War II period from 16 February 1944 through 9 May 1946. Following is the justification that was written by the Headquarters, 2174th USA Garrison Commander, Col. Lyle N. Garrett, Jr. to award the Superior Civilian Service Award: "Mr. Lovelace's knowledge in the budget monitoring area enabled him to perform with a high degree of proficiency. Mr. Lovelace displays outstanding technical knowledge and professional ability in the management of government funds. He has demonstrated the ability to accomplish the task of fulfilling both roles as Staff Operations and Training Technician and Assistant Supervisor Staff Administrator by relying on the many positive experiences and abilities which has developed over his tenure of thirty-seven years. His total dedication and loyalty to the service of the United States Army has been remark-

able. Mr. Lovelace's initiative, enthusiasm and ability to excel in his field has distinguished him. His handling of funds for Headquarters, 2174th US Army Garrison and seven subordinate units are held in high regard by the 80th Division (Training) and has been recommended by Division Internal Review Board that no changes be made in his management of funds. His tact and diplomacy in dealing with budgetary matters are absolutely superior. He is always willing to go beyond that which is normally expected of him and has proven beyond a doubt that he is a true professional in all respects. This award only modestly expresses his contribution to the United States Army Reserves and his country. Mr. Lovelace is not only a credit to himself, but also to the unit and the United States."

$1,000.00 was awarded by the 80th Division in honor of budgetary and training accomplishments.

My retirement was with three creditable careers: Army Reserve, Insurance and Civil service. I think one must make things happen especially as far as work is concerned including managing your own career, ensuring you are current with knowledge and skills, and "tooting your own horn" if necessary. I learned early in life to be self sufficient and to routinely save for the future.

During my Army Reserve career, I never used a day of sick leave, and over my entire career only 14 sick days were utilized: 7 for a hemorrhoid operation; 2 days due to food poisoning, and 5 days for roseola during basic training. If I've counted correctly, over a fifty-eight year work career, I missed only 14 days due to sickness. I am very proud of this achievement.

THE IMPORTANCE
OF EDUCATION

When I entered the workforce education was less important than mechanical skills in obtaining jobs. The requirement for educational achievement began to make its mark on my life during WWII. Just shortly after finishing Army basic training I enrolled and completed a course in Air Force Administration School at Drew Field Army Base. My next educational move was to finish high school. While working at the Veteran's Administration, I went to Jefferson Senior High School in Roanoke to finish grades seven through twelve. I received my high school diploma in 1953 at the age of 27. The teachers were extremely supportive and encouraging. They worked with me to complete the courses needed for a diploma. These teachers wanted me to succeed and had a large positive impact on the quality of my future and the lives of my children. There was not a GED (general equivalency diploma) test back in those days so without

LOVELACE, ROBERT—"Nothing is impossible to a willing heart."

H.S. Graduation in 1953

teachers willing to work with me to take courses on an accelerated basis at Jefferson Senior High School I could not have obtained my diploma. I am thankful for the commitment of those teachers!

Since the war disrupted many soldier's educational endeavors the US government following WWII introduced the GI-Bill. This program provided monetary assistance to veterans to help them continue and finish their education. While working full-time at Burlington, I began using my GI-Bill. In 1953 and 1954 I attended National Business College and studied Accounting and Business Administration. In my case the GI-Bill was a great help, but the juggling of home, work and school was treacherous. When my shift at Burlington ended at 6:50 A.M., I would then hurry over to National Business College and attend classes and study from 8 A.M. to 3 P.M. After school I would rush home to eat and sleep and then get up at 10 P.M. to get ready and be at work at 11 P.M. A six day cycle of this intensity was an extremely difficult schedule to keep. On one occasion I injured a finger at work. I remember having to change the dressing while driving home since there was no extra time at home to spare before heading off to school. Occasionally, I recall having to do a little speeding to make it all work. To keep the police at bay I would frequently change my highway route between home and work. In class I would often dose-off at my desk and drop a book or something. My professor, Mr. Townsend, knew my situation so he rarely gave me a hard time. Once he was giving the class an accounting examination and I was way ahead of schedule, so I put my head down on my desk for a short rest and unintentionally fell asleep. When I woke-up the exam was over and I failed to complete the exam. When the professor came by to pick-up the exam he said: "I see Mr. Lovelace, you, are not afraid of work because you will lie down beside it and go to sleep!" I had to wait a couple of weeks but he allowed me to re-take the exam. Even with such a rigorous schedule I was able to make the Dean's List two or three times, but I was unable to finish the degree program because I'd used up my GI Bill and did not have the extra money for tuition and books. Below is a recap of my schooling since leaving college in 1954:

- 1960, Army Administration Training
- 1971, second Army Administration Training course at Fort Benjamin, Harrison, IN
- 1979 and 1981, Reserve Technician Course in Richmond, VA
- 1985, Management Strategy Tactic and Development Course, Roanoke, VA
- 1986, Data Processing at Virginia Western Community College, Roanoke, VA (using a personal computer for the first time at age 60)
- 1988, Unit Management Course at Fort McCoy, WI
- 1989, Mobilization and Planning Course at Fort McCoy, WI.

Family 1951

Family 1972

CHAPTER 5

OUR FAMILY

Janice and I had four children:

- Janet Diane, born in 1949
- Robert Ashley, born in 1951
- Debra Lynn, born in 1956
- David Jeffrey, born in 1960.

Each child's two given-names came about as Janice would pick one name and I would pick the other which was combined. Janice and I did the best we knew how to raise our children. We passed on a value driven life, strong work ethic, and giving to others while living a Christian life. We provided love, encouragement, discipline and hard-work to meet their needs. We also added some niceties to their and our lives as well. Our daughters and youngest son took piano lessons for several years. Robert Ashley was on the school wrestling team. David was in the Boy Scouts. One extravagant gift was the purchase of a TV set shortly after a television station (I believe WSLS) came to Roanoke. The TV was of course a black and white set and cost about $500. In 1952, the purchase was a huge splurge when our household income was only $100 per week. That old TV in our early years as a family provided loads of entertainment and enjoyment! I also think often of our family trips and vacations together. Going to Florida was one of our favorite vacations. Other great places where we traveled to were: the Smithsonian Institute in Washington, D.C., Endless Caverns in Luray, VA, Great Smokey Mountains in TN and NC, Amish Country in Lancaster, PA, Hershey Park and the Chocolate Factory at Hershey, PA. We also traveled to Lookout Mountain near Chattanooga, TN, the Biltmore Estates in Asheville, NC, Myrtle Beach, SC, Virginia Beach, VA, Maggie Valley in NC, Indianapolis Speedway in IN, and once we traveled all the way to New Orleans, LA. I also recall the family coming to visit me on weekends at the Army Reserve training at Fort Meade, MD, Fort Lee, VA and Fort Picket, VA.

CHILDREN GROWING-UP

Both Robert Ashley and David Jeffrey began delivering newspapers about the age of 12 and continued to do so until they reached the age of 16. Some days when I didn't have to work myself, I would help them. Janice would also sometimes help by pulling the paper wagon or driving them in the car. The only requirement I made in their delivering papers was when payday came, each had to place $5 in a savings account. The rest of their pay could be spent as they wished. After the paper-route both boys found other temporary jobs after school. By the time driving age came each had enough saved to buy a used car. I recall on one occasion that Robert Ashley became upset with me because I had discouraged his purchase of an old Corvette that I believed to be mechanically unsound. When we went together to see the car the owner was unable to start the car. Seems he pushed and pulled the car all over southeast Roanoke but it just wouldn't start. When we left I told the owner if he got the car started to give me a call. Sometime later he called and told me the car was now running. Again we went to see the car but received some discouraging news from the mechanic who had worked on the car. He told me when he worked on the car he had removed the clutch throwout bushing and beat the bushing with a hammer to make it swell to the proper size. This solidified my concern that the car would be nothing but problems, so I told Robert Ashley he could not buy the car.

Janet Diane went from high school into nurses' resident training and married just after graduation. She did not buy a car. Debra Lynn bought a used Mercury Cougar and kept it for awhile before trading-up for a better car. Since mechanical work is a necessity on most used cars, I endeavored to help my kids either make the repairs or sometimes helped with repair cost.

I recall buying an old antique Studebaker from a man in Wytheville, VA. I brought it home and stored it in a shed at Mr. France's home directly behind our house. One day Mr. France's son came over and said that I needed to move that "piece of junk" out of his father's shed. I took exception to his remark and walked over to see the car. I discovered that Robert Ashley and some friends had taken the radio out through the dashboard and had broken the headlights and other lights. Mr. France's son was right: the car did look like a piece of junk. I hated the loss because of the value of the car and let Robert Ashley know of my disappointment in him. I chalked-up the loss and incident to immaturity and adolescent growing pains.

Janet Diane graduated from Roanoke Memorial Hospital School of Nursing and served in R.N. and supervisory positions in a variety of clinical disciplines. She married a wonderfully nice man who has a degree in electrical engineering. Robert Ashley, who has a college degree in business, married a lady from Florida who is a fine vocalist. Robert Ashley served as a transportation director for the Norfolk Southern Corporation. Debra Lynn holds a bachelor's degree in accounting and a master's degree in human resources; she worked in various positions including Senior HR Director and held a Certified Public Accountant designation. She married a fine man who has a college degree in business. David Jeffrey graduated with a degree in computer science, obtained multiple information systems certifications and worked for ITG in Lorton, VA. I am glad to say I have three grandchildren: J.R., Christin and Scott, and six great grandchildren: Danielle, Shane, Quinn, Adalyn, Kensley and Aliza, and one great great grandchild: Destiny.

MY BELOVED JANICE

I have said lots about my work, life experiences and other things but little about Janice. What's notable about Janice is her big heart and how she was a great encourager. She allowed the children freedom to make many of their own decisions using the values they had been taught. While I was working long hours, the children had devotions at home and participated in choir, the Royal Ambassadors (R.A.), Girl's Auxiliary (G.A.) and other church activities. Janice took the children to minister to elderly ladies in the church congregation and our neighborhood. Janice and the children would take the widowed ladies to get groceries, to the bank and post office and to most any other place they needed to go. While visiting residents of nursing homes, Janice would ask the nursing staff about residents who rarely had visitors. She and the children would visit these often lonely and forgotten people. I must say Janice was the better part of our marriage, carrying the load at home with her health issues while I had all those extra jobs and was furthering my education. She always gave me great advice when I struggled with life's issues.

Janice developed a career with the American Red Cross. Following her heart, she established a local Prisoner of War (POW) Chapter in Roanoke, Virginia. She frequently visited the Bland Correctional Prison to help prisoners and their families qualify for benefits. Working in southwestern Virginia, she assisted homeless veterans and their families in finding temporary aid. It was a surprise to walk with her in downtown Roanoke and hear the homeless men call out to her, "Mrs. Lovelace, Mrs. Lovelace, Hello! It's good to see you! Thanks for your help!"

You see they knew how much she cared and appreciated all that she attempted to do for them. I think Janice's drive and desire was from the heart while mine was more out of necessity. I know when she left this world the Lord got a saint and now she's waiting for me to come see her in heaven! My beloved Janice passed away on April 18, 2005.

Sergeant Major Lovelace at retirement

CHAPTER 6

RETIREMENT & REMEMBERING

THE OLD TROUTDALE FARM

The old log barn, tobacco barn, and the tenant house have long been gone. My father had removed the lumber in the original barn and built a barn with three stalls and a mow overhead. Due to years of weathering the recycled barn is gone. In 1994 my brother, Donald, my son David, and I made repairs to the foundation and floor of the granary and put-on a new galvanized metal roof. The old house also has a new roof, storm windows and bathroom addition, but is still in need of new weather-board siding and paint. The old farmhouse, woodshed and granary remained standing until the mid 2000s when a fire occurred after the property was sold. All fences are gone and the yard and the surrounding area is overgrown with trees and brush. Three apple trees remain in the orchard.

THE POW CAMP IN 1995

In October 1995, Janice and I drove through the Drew Field Army Base POW Camp in Florida. After 50 years many things had changed and I recognized little, mostly because most of the old wooden buildings were gone. The only building left was the officer's club on the edge of Kingsley Lake. The camp at that time was in the hands of the Florida National Guard who had built a new headquarters and other cinder block buildings on the property.

WAR IS HELL

I often think of those who served in the war but did not survive. One was a first cousin named Breece. Our family gatherings were never quite the same without Breece. Today we hear lots of criticism for the US using the atomic bomb during the war, but when I think of the many lives saved by shortening the war on both sides I can only affirm that our leaders took the appropriate measures.

RECONNECTING WITH OLD ARMY BUDDIES & FRIENDS

As mentioned earlier my best Army buddy was Jadie Williams. Over the years I lost contact with Jadie, so after retirement in 1995 I spent a lot of time trying to locate him. I made contact with some of my other Army buddies whose addresses I had kept and asked them if they had heard from or knew what happened to Jadie. None of them could tell me anything about Jadie. I was able to locate Betty Rosen through her brother James who lived in Tampa. James gave me Betty's phone number but didn't have any information on Jadie. I called Betty who updated me on her life since we went our separate ways after the war. Betty had married in 1952 but her husband had died of cancer in 1994. She had one son who also lived in Florida near her. Her sister Dorothy had brain cancer and was living near Phoenix, Arizona. At the time Betty was preparing to go visit Dorothy who was not expected to survive the cancer. Betty's mother, Mrs. Rosen had died in 1988 and her brother Lewis had died of a heart attack a few years before that. She had not heard from Jadie since her mother died but she felt most probably he had already passed-on. I called Betty back in August 1995 and learned that Dorothy had died. On a trip to Florida in October 1995, Janice and I stopped by Betty's home in Tampa to visit. Betty was as gracious and friendly as ever and we had a wonderful time together. She told us how she really loved and missed her husband. After we talked a while the three of us went out to a restaurant where over a marvelous seafood dinner we continued our talk of old-times. That was the last time I saw my wonderful friend Betty. I continued searching for Jadie and finally located his son through an internet search. I then wrote his son who responded in December 1996. I regret that I did not look for Jadie earlier because he told me that Jadie had died in 1981. I guess life simply had gotten in the way.

EDUCATIONAL REGRETS & LIFE EXPERIENCE

My regret comes later in life and is of my own making. A better education would have possibly provided better support to my own family especially in providing more dollars toward their educational needs. Education is knowledge and knowledge opens doors to better careers. I suppose that I could have reduced living expenses with a smaller family but I would have missed God's blessing. I love all my children and grandchildren and there's not one I could give up. My hope for their future was bolstered by my own parents' example, which was typical of their hardy generation and generations before them. Respectfully, my parents were ill educated to adjust to a world changing more rapidly than ever before. My father as a boy plowed with yoked oxen, yet he lived to see men sent into space. Mother who was reared and trained for farming life in the fashion of her time went beyond that because she had little choice. My parents stayed together, held the family together and passed on "deposits of their personal steel". They both could have done little more but more importantly we children had a solid example to follow. You can mark me down as an old fogy, but this country has grown soft and spoiled. Today's psychologists and sociologists say that if you have certain things happen to you, then you must have been abused or mistreated as a child. Too much today is based on some-type of child abuse in rearing which has supposedly resulted in one's deficiencies in their adult conduct. Our justice system today is sympathetic to these espoused beliefs and many criminal actions are going unpunished. I'm not saying that one's child-hood circumstances are not part of their underlying issues. However, blaming others does not relieve one of being responsible, good and honest citizens.

A PAUSE FOR CORRECTION

In closing I wish to reflect on a personal issue with author-writer, Kemp Battle Nye who wrote a book in 1993 titled: *Ripshin.*[9] In this work Nye wrote authoritatively on the treatment of black convicts and other blacks who were supposed to have lived in or near Troutdale. The book's beginning implies that Nye's resource for factualness was author Sherwood Anderson who wrote and spent a good deal of time at his cabin at his Ripshin Farm near Troutdale. The book becomes fiction and looses credibility as there were no black people that lived in Troutdale. There were a few black convicts working on State Route 16 in 1934 which was to pass through Troutdale. My recollection of these chain-gang blacks is that there were neither issues nor problems.

EPILOGUE

I have covered a lot of territory since September 9, 1925. I am now 97 years young with a sound mind and aging body. All that physical work, fresh air from the farm, quitting smoking, finding humor in daily life, and now taking 30 pills a day, helped me with longevity. My wife and siblings have all passed away, but my children and grandchildren are with me. I have lived at a number of places and made many friends. I have also made many mistakes! There are people who shape their lives by the fear of death and others who shape their lives through thanks-

Robert, 2010

giving, joy and satisfaction in life. The former live dying and the latter die living. This is not to say that I never ponder death. I often have said in my later years: "I just forgot to get old, so I will not worry about it." I know death will come someday because God designed both life and death with eternal life coming on the heels of physical death. I've had a great life and a wonderful family and I know Jesus is preparing for me a home in heaven where I'll spend eternity. I'm not going anywhere until I get the call but I'll only make one last move which is not too far in the future to a mansion not made with human hands. The Bible tells me of this most wonderful place where there will be no more sickness nor pain, no more sorrow, and no more separation. I will not have to worry about the light bill, the water bill, the food bill, the grocery bill and all other bills because I won't need this world's goods. There I'll be with Janice who was the love of my life on earth for 57 years, with my family and friends and other wonderful people for all eternity, and with the one that built the mansion and invited me to come. I accepted his generous offer to come and be with him in that fantastic city. If you don't know whom I'm talking about, His name is Jesus Christ! So keep on the sunny-side, and I hope to see you there someday! Oh by the way, I hope to see old Jadie there too!

ROBERT J. LOVELACE
6/1/2006, 9/22/2020,
1/21/2022, 7/1/2022

ENDNOTES

1   Benjamin Floyd Nuckolls, *Pioneer Settlers of Grayson County*, 1979 ed. (Bristol: King Print. Co., 1914), 3.

2   A face cord is a rack of wood eight feet long and four feet high and could be any length up to about eighteen inches.

3   A flail is a wooden tool with a heavy club like end, called a swiple, attached with a leather strip to a long handle or staff. If a leather strip was not available, one could take a hammer and beat a place about eighteen inches from the largest end until it was bruised and thin enough to bend.

A flail constructed in this manner would not last very long. Of course any grain could be thrashed this way.

4   Winnowing occurs on a windy day when the grain was put into a container and while holding it high, was poured out very slowly on a tarpaulin. As the grain fell the wind would blow the chaff from it leaving the grain clean.

5   An evaporator was made by putting sheet metal on top and bottom of a rectangle made of wood about four feet wide and eight feet long with some water added to produce steam. A hole about one and one half inch was cut in the top of the sheet metal to add water and an apple was placed over the hole to keep the steam in. This apple served as a safety valve. A furnace was made with stones and mud

about the same size as the evaporator, with a short chimney at one end to give it draft so the fire would burn and to dissipate the smoke. If the evaporator got too much steam it would blow the apple off and let the steam out without causing damage to the evaporator.

6   A hammer mill's purpose is to shred or crush aggregate material into smaller pieces by the repeated blows of little hammers.

7   The cogs in the cane mill caused the rollers to turn together. One of the rollers had a long shaft protruding out the top to hook the sweep to. A sweep is a long heavy pole about thirty feet in length and about eight inches at the butt. It is balanced by putting the shaft at the center of gravity of the pole so that there will be less side pressure on the rollers. A hole

about two inches in diameter is mortised in the butt of the sweep and a lead pole is attached. A horse is hooked to the small end of the sweep and a lead line from the horse is hooked to the lead pole. This leads the horse in a circle of about forty feet.

8   A homemade sled was made by taking an eight-inch wide plank and from it cutting two, four-foot pieces to make the main-sled runners. The runners were tapered on one end about twenty degrees with cross pieces of plank about twenty-four inches long nailed across the top of each runner. This completed the main sled. Now a guide-sled had to be made. Making the guide-sled was done by creating a shorter version of the main-sled but only about eighteen inches long. A hole was bored in the center of the front cross

piece of the main-sled and back piece of the guide-sled. A board about three inches wide and about twenty inches long with a hole bored in each end was then loosely bolted to each sled. The guide-sled provided steering to the main-sled.

9   Kemp Battle Nye, *Ripshin*, (Carrboro: Signal Books Co.,1993).

Robert and Janice in 1972

THROUGH

THE YEARS

Robert and his three sisters early 1930s

Robert and his siblings late 1940s

Siblings and parents 1950s

Robert's Siblings 1960s

Robert's parents 1960s

Siblings and mother 1970s

Siblings 1997

Family 1951

Family 1972

Family 1980s

Family 1997 and 50 year anniversary